Met[illegible]lastics

Contents

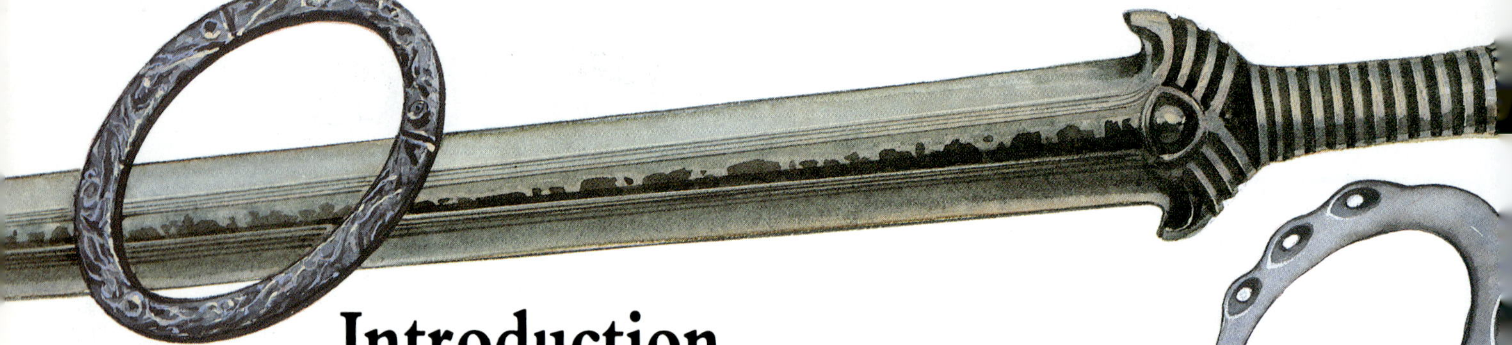

Introduction

Look around you. How many metals can you see? They are everywhere, from the can of cola you might have when you get home to the catches on your bedroom windows; from the tiny eyelets that your laces go through in your shoes to the money jangling in your pocket; from the lorry thundering past on the nearest main road to the brake handle on your bike; from the tools of the surgeon in a hospital to the microphones used by your favourite rock group on stage.

Because they are so important to us now it's easy to forget that many metals have been used by people on the Earth for thousands of years. You might hear people talk of 'The Bronze Age'. They are describing a time when people discovered how to make bronze by mixing copper and tin. This was an important breakthrough; bronze was hard enough to be used for shaping other metals. There are other ages too. If you ever hear people talking about 'The Iron Age', it is because they are describing a time which began over three thousand years ago when people first discovered iron and how to use it, at first for simple tools but later for more complicated things.

Since those times, new metals have been discovered and new **alloys** — mixtures of different metals — have been developed. Each has its own special properties and its own special uses. Each is good in some ways and poor in others.

In a few hundred years' time, people may look back and try to describe the times we are living in now and call them 'The Plastics Age'. Plastic is a relatively new invention, developed from our growing understanding of the properties of oil. We have only used it for about the last fifty years. This may seem a long time to you but just compare it with the thousands of years people have used metals.

Our understanding of plastic may still be very limited. Just as new metals were discovered and new alloys developed, new ways of producing and using different plastics are being found. Plastic is a

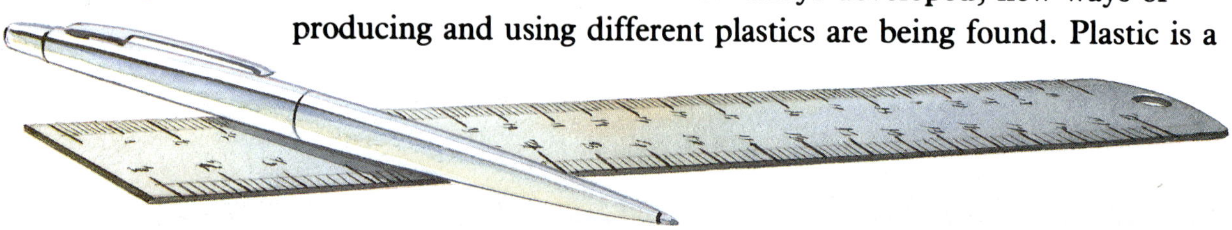

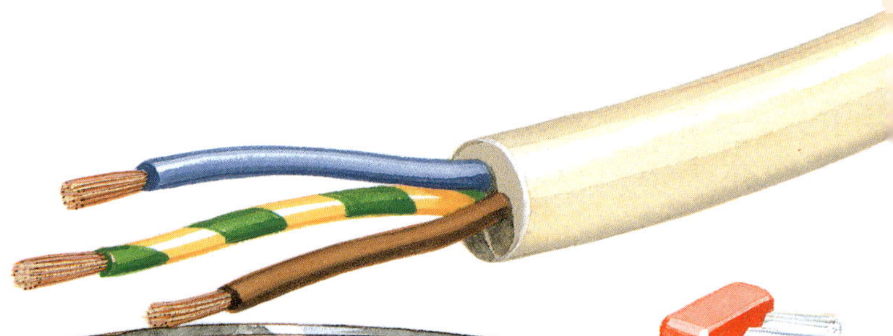

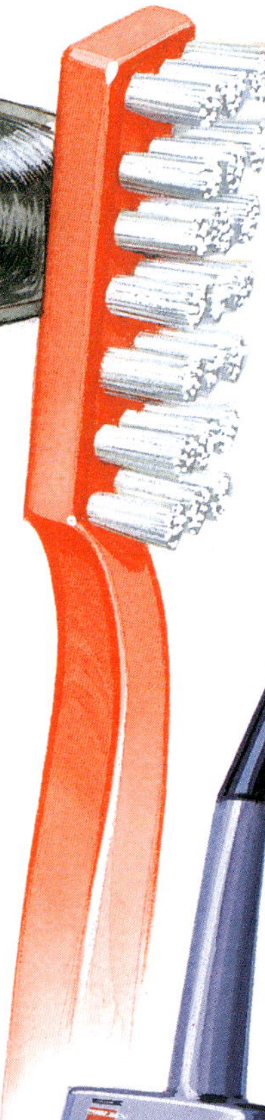

very exciting material. It can be produced in very thin sheets or great thick blocks; it can be easily shaped and coloured; and it can be soft and delicate or hard and very strong. Just think of your lunch box, the dustpan and brush in the corner of your classroom or the wheels on your roller-skates. Plastics can often replace metals.

When plastic was first used, though, it wasn't that successful. It broke easily or wore out very quickly. People often think of it as a cheap substitute for metal and make remarks such as, 'It's quite nice, but it's only plastic'.

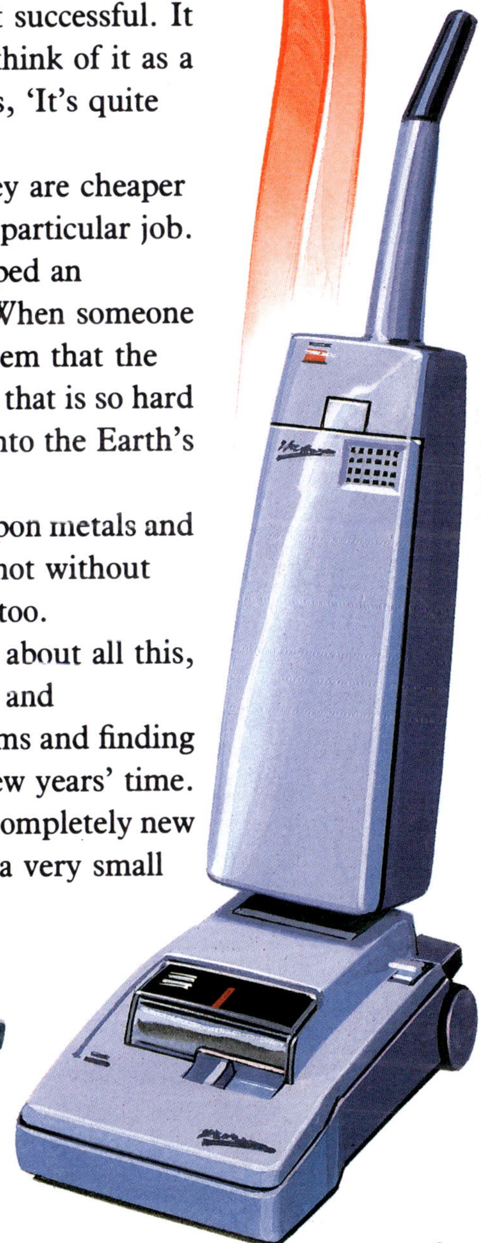

Some plastics may still be used simply because they are cheaper than metal even if they're not always suitable for the particular job. In the last fifty years, though, scientists have developed an astonishing range of plastics to suit most purposes. When someone next says to you, 'It's only plastic', you might tell them that the rocket heads of many spaceships are made of a plastic that is so hard that it can withstand the enormous heat of re-entry into the Earth's atmosphere better than almost any metal.

This book is all about the way we use and depend upon metals and plastics. For all the benefits they bring, their use is not without problems and you will find out about some of those too.

At the very same moment that you are finding out about all this, scientists will be working to improve our knowledge and understanding of these materials, developing new forms and finding new uses. You could be one of those scientists in a few years' time. You may even be a part of the team which develops a completely new material which replaces both metals and plastics. In a very small way, you can begin to think about it now.

What is a metal?

Metals are not always easy to identify. You could use the following list of common characteristics to help:

- cold to touch
- shiny
- hard
- a distinctive ring when struck
- bends
- conducts heat easily
- conducts electricity easily
- mixes to form alloys

Have you ever thought about how many everyday objects are made of metal? Have a look around your classroom, your school and your home. You can even have a look at yourself — look at your clothing, for example, and in your pockets!

You may find coins or keys in your pockets. You might be wearing a badge which has a metal back and pin to it. If you wear glasses, you'll probably find they've got some metal in them somewhere. The zip fasteners on your anorak may be plastic but most zips still have a metal pull. If you are wearing shoes with laces, you may find the laces have metal ends.

What about the tables you sit at? Which parts of these are metal? What about the rest of the furniture and fittings? In how many different places can you find metal being used?

On your way home, look and touch to find out how many of the different things you pass, or use, contain metal.

Look in one room at home and note all the places where metal is used. Other members of your group could choose different rooms in their homes to do this. As a group, you can then compare the uses of metals in different types of rooms.

Why do you think we use so much metal?

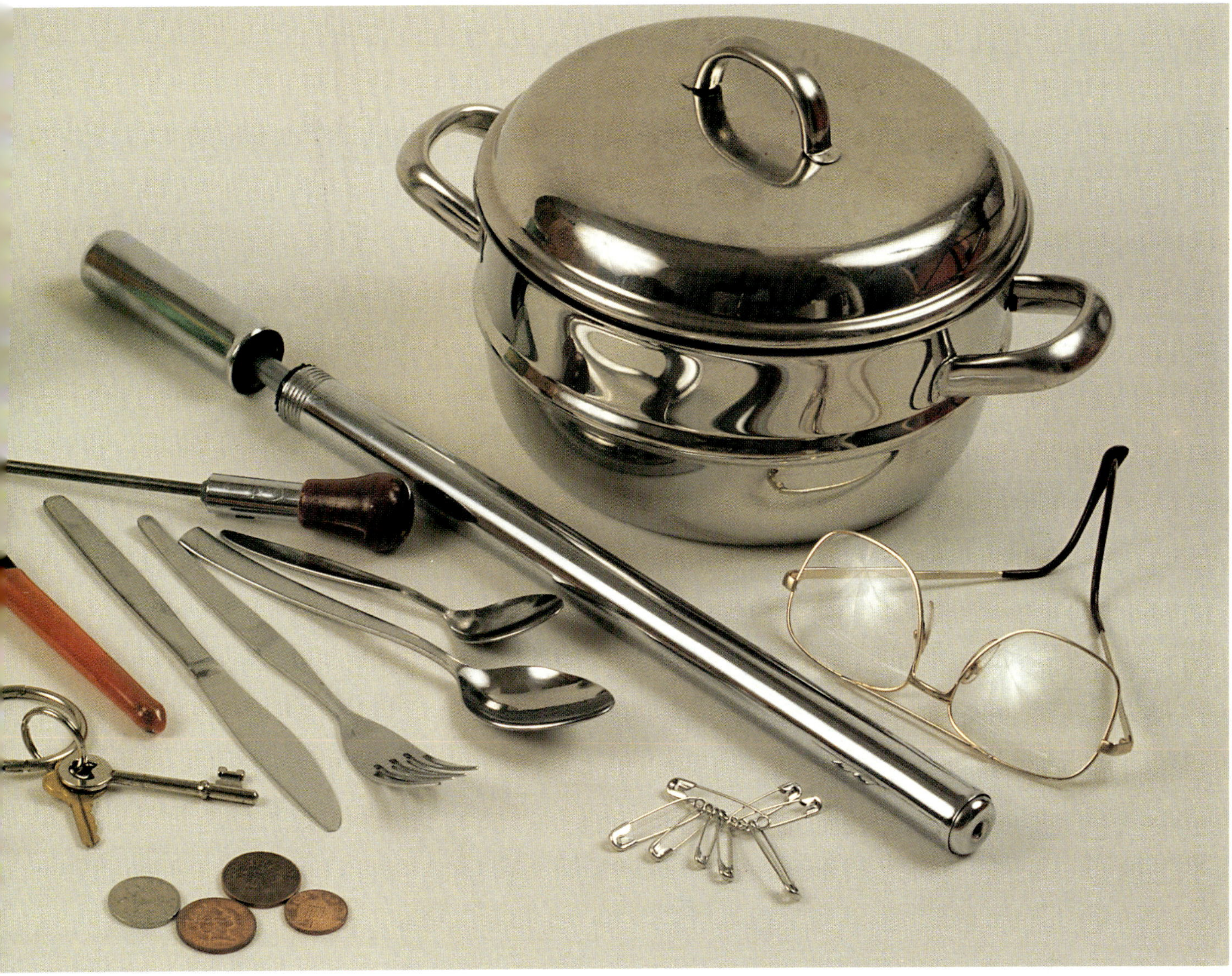

Where do metals come from?

Very few metals can be found in their pure form. Most have to be extracted from minerals.

Minerals come from boiling magma, the layer of molten rock that churns away beneath the Earth's cold, rocky crust. Magma forces its way up towards the surface wherever there is a weakness — through a volcano, for example. When hot magma liquid is trapped in a pool or forced along a crack, it cools to leave mineral-rich deposits in the rock. This process has been happening for millions of years. Deposits which contain large quantities of minerals concentrated in one place are known as ores.

Geologists are people who study rock formations. They work out where ore is most likely to be found. That place is then tested by drilling into the ground. If ore is found, the area can then be mined. Once the ore has been dug out of the ground, it is crushed and separated to take the valuable minerals from it. These minerals are then treated so that metal can be extracted.

Some minerals, such as many copper and aluminium ores, are close to the surface of the Earth. They can be scraped up from open mines. Deeper mineral deposits have to be mined by blasting and tunnelling deep into the rock. The deepest mines in the world are gold mines.

The entrance to a gold mine

Rivers which flow through mineral-rich rocks can wash tiny fragments of metal out of the rock. When fresh deposits of gold were found in California and Australia in the last century, there was a 'Gold Rush' as hundreds of prospectors travelled there to make their fortunes. Many spent long hours standing in streams, endlessly sifting and ***panning*** *the river-bed sand and silt, hoping to make their fortunes from the gold they were trying to find.*

Open cast iron ore mine in Australia

Gold miner underground

Enormous amounts of ore have to be dug up and separated to obtain a useful amount of metal. When a new mineral deposit is found, mining companies have to be sure that extracting the metal will make them a profit as mining operations are expensive and dangerous. Nowadays, though, the supplies of cheap, easily extracted minerals are dwindling so more difficult mines, often with smaller amounts of ore, are being worked. The Romans mined lead in the United Kingdom and left large 'spoil' heaps. Many of these have been reworked and a lot of lead has been found in them which had not been taken out by the Romans.

In the past, huge areas of land have been spoiled by mining operations. Today, though, mining companies realize how important it is to conserve land, as well as the Earth's supply of rare minerals.

Ancient Egyptians used meteorite iron to make jewellery (about 3500 BC).

Around 2000 BC, people in Europe made bronze by mixing copper and tin. They made bronze weapons, jewellery and cutlery.

Around 1400 BC, people called Hittites who liv in Asia, learned how to work iron ore at high temperatures to make hard, strong weapons ar tools.

The history of metals

Before metals were discovered, people used tools and weapons made of stone, wood or bone for everything — fighting and hunting, farming, cooking and building. They shaped pots and bricks from clay and used fire to harden them. However, people were always searching for new and better materials that did not break or burn, or go blunt so easily.

Occasionally, someone may have found a piece of metal — a sparkling nugget of gold or silver, a lump of 'raw' copper, or a piece of iron from one of the many meteorites that have struck the Earth from space. Here at last was a material that did not quickly wear away with use, soften in rain or water, or burn up and crack in the fire like wood or stone. In fact, heating metal and hammering it into shape produced a stronger material.

People found that melted, or molten, metals could be mixed together to make new metals which we call alloys. When copper, for example, is mixed with tin, it makes an alloy called bronze which is very strong. The discovery of bronze changed many people's lives. Hard bronze tools could be used to shape other materials and armies equipped with bronze weapons and armour were very powerful.

The search for more useful metals and alloys continued, surrounded by secrecy, mystery and magic, until around 1000 BC. Then bronze gave way to iron which is still the most used metal today. Iron has many advantages over bronze: it is cheaper; it is less likely to crack or break; and it can be given a sharper edge.

Much hotter furnaces called blast furnaces enabled iron to be melted, poured into moulds and cast. However, supplies of charcoal, the fuel used in the furnace, were limited because the timber used to make charcoal was needed for shipbuilding.

There were unsuccessful attempts at using coal as a replacement for charcoal to **smelt** iron. Impurities in the coal were given off during the smelting process which affected the composition and strength of the iron.

Large quantities of cheap, strong, metal building materials revolutionized building, transport and engineering.

The first steel alloys were produced about 200 BC. An alloy is a mixture of metals. Steel alloys were used to make strong, sharp swords that could cut through bronze and iron weapons and armour. The secret of steel-making was then lost or forgotten for many hundreds of years.

Wrought iron was made by heating iron in a furnace or forge. The temperature was raised using large bellows. Hot metal was bent and beaten into bars, forged and shaped into tools, weapons and machinery.

In 1709, at Coalbrookdale in Shropshire, Abraham Darby and his family adapted the blast furnace using coke, made from coal, as the fuel instead of coal. Coke has fewer impurities than coal so it can help to produce better iron.

The blast furnace method was improved. Mass production of cast iron began.

In the 1800s, the Bessemer convertor was developed for bulk conversion of iron into steel. This was the first successful method of making large quantities of steel at low cost and led to the widespread use of steel in building, transport, tools, machinery and weapons.

During the 20th century, steel manufacturing has improved with more efficient processing methods.

How iron and steel are made

Tapping a blast furnace

Iron

The iron that is used in metal-working and to make alloys comes from iron ore that is found in rocks under the Earth's surface. Iron ore is a combination of iron, carbon, oxygen and silicon. The iron ore has to be heated at a very high temperature in a furnace to melt the iron in it so that this iron can be extracted. This process is called smelting.

First, the crushed ore is mixed with crushed limestone and coke and put in the furnace. Then hot air is blasted through the base of the furnace. This causes the coke to burn fiercely which melts the metal in the ore. It runs to the bottom of the furnace where it is collected.

The silicon and other impurities from the ore combine with the limestone and float on top of the molten iron. This is called slag and it is discarded in heaps near the metalworks. Carbon dioxide gas is also produced during this process and escapes from the furnace through chimneys.

Steelworks in South Wales

Pouring steel into moulds

Steel bar coming out of the rolling mill

Steel

Steel is made by heating molten iron and steel scrap and blasting oxygen through it to burn away the carbon and impurities it contains. This gives off a huge spray of gas and sparks. The molten steel is poured into a giant ladle where other additives are mixed with it. The steel is poured into huge moulds where it sets into ingots. It can also be cast as thin sheets.

Other metals can be added to produce steel with special properties — high strength, flexibility, resistance to rusting, shock or heat, for example.

The hardness and other properties of the steel produced are also varied by heating and cooling treatment. Over two thousand years ago, swordmakers in Spain, Syria and Japan knew how to produce strong, sharp blades by dipping red-hot steel into cold liquid. This produced steel which was easy to shape and was not brittle.

Choosing the right metal

Most metals have three things in common: they are all shiny; they all allow heat and electricity to pass through them; and they can all be mixed together to form useful alloys.

There are thousands of different alloys, each with its own special 'recipe' and properties. They have been developed over centuries by **metallurgists** to create the best material for a particular job. When builders, engineers and designers choose a metal or alloy, they select the one with the best properties at the right price. They have to ask questions like these about the metal:

- Will it be strong enough without being too heavy or too light?
- How easily can it be shaped?
- Is it magnetic?
- How easily does it conduct electricity?
- How will heat affect it?
- How expensive will it be?

Strength

The strength of a metal is not just how much weight it can carry but also how well it stands up to constant bending or vibrations. Does it bend before breaking or does it crack and give way suddenly?

Weight

Lead and tungsten are heavy metals. Aluminium and magnesium are light and strong. These light metals are being used more and more to build cars, lorries and other vehicles. Why do you think this is?

Corrosion

Many metals do not last for a long time. They are altered or eaten away by other substances such as air and water. This process is called corrosion. Other metals, like aluminium and copper, react with oxygen to produce a substance called an **oxide** which creates a protective layer on the surface of the metal. In iron and steel, however, the reaction continues and eats away, or corrodes, them. Longer-lasting steel is made by alloying it with nickel to make stainless steel.

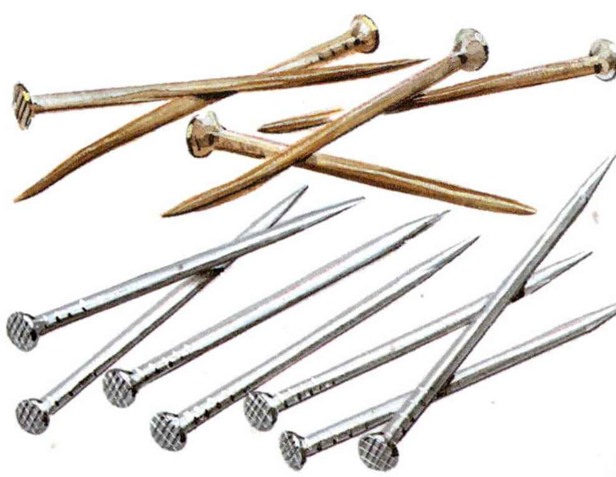

Colour and shine
Nearly all metals are a silvery grey colour. Glittering yellow gold and fiery reddish copper are two exceptions. All metals shine when the surface is smoothed and polished, especially the softer ones. Many metals go dull when they are exposed to the air.

Hardness
The softer the metal, the quicker it wears away with use. Most metals can be strengthened and made harder by mixing them with another metal. Copper and tin are both soft but mix together to make bronze which is an alloy hard enough to make engine parts.

Expansion
Metals expand at different rates when they heat up. In the cold, they contract. Mercury is a liquid metal which expands and shrinks and is used in thermometers to measure changes in temperature.

Melting point
Each metal and alloy melts at a particular temperature. Lead and tin have low melting points and are used to make solder for joining metal pipes and wires. Tungsten has the highest melting point and is used for tools which can get very hot when they are being used and for the **filaments** in light bulbs which also get very hot.

Heat conductivity
All metals allow heat to pass through them. Copper and aluminium are both excellent heat conductors. They are used in heating systems and for making saucepans.

Electrical conductivity
Silver and copper are good electrical conductors. Most electric wiring is made from copper. Aluminium is also used because it is lighter and cheaper than silver and copper.

Magnetism
Iron, nickel and cobalt are all magnetic but copper and aluminium are not.

Radioactivity
A few metals such as uranium and radium give off radiation. The nuclear energy they create is an important source of power. In certain circumstances, radiation can be very dangerous.

Testing metals

Look around you. How many different metals can you find? Remember, you may be carrying metals around with you. Coins, belt buckles, watches, glasses, pens and even combs can be metal. Make a collection of different metals.

Most metals share similar qualities but there are some differences. The results of these tests might surprise you.

Are all metals shiny?

- Try shining some coins. Use some small change — pennies, five and ten pence pieces.
- Try using different 'polishers' and cloths; you could use brass or silver polish, salt, lemon juice, vinegar, bicarbonate of soda (on a damp rag) and polishing cloths of soft cloth, leather or wool.
- Which gives the best shine?
- Can you make the coins shine like new?
- What do you think you are rubbing away?

Are all metals magnetic?

- Use a magnet to test your metals. Try your coins, 'tin' cans, door handles, pipes and taps. Do **not** try anything electrical — or your watch! (Many modern watches contain tiny magnets which can be damaged by larger magnets. Wind-up watches can be damaged too.)
- Are all metals magnetic?
- Are metals magnetic even when they are painted?
- Are metals magnetic when they are covered in plastic. Try testing a plastic-covered steel coat-hanger.
- Tin cans are made of steel coated in tin. What is the tin for? Is it the tin or the steel that is magnetic? How can you find out?
- Some soft drinks cans are made of steel, others are made of aluminium; can you tell them apart with a magnet?

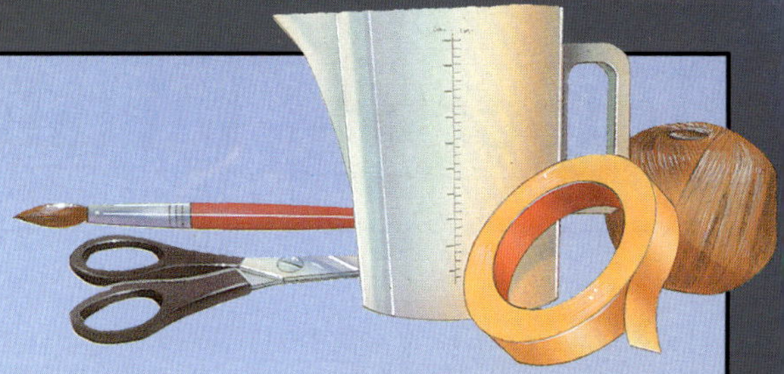

Hot or cold?

Metals often feel cold to the touch. Touch your metals. Are they cold?

Metals quickly take, or conduct, the heat of your body away. Touch metals with your fingertips and the heat is conducted away. Your fingertips feel cold. You can try this test to see if metals are better conductors of heat than other materials:

- Put some long objects — an old pencil, a plastic comb, a metal knitting needle and a piece of wire coat-hanger — into hot (not boiling) water. Try to find objects which are all about the same length to make the test as fair as possible.
- Touch the ends with your fingertips. Which is the first to conduct the heat to your finger? (You can also try this test with several different metals to find out if some metals are better conductors of heat than others.)

Metals conduct electricity — or do they?

- Try putting different metals in an electric circuit. You can try tin foil, coins, different wires, paper-clips, pins and drawing-pins — but not your watch! Put them between the bulb and the battery. Will the bulb light up?
- Does metal coated with plastic or thick paint conduct electricity? Try to find out. You could use a plastic-covered steel coat-hanger.

Important metals and alloys

Metal	Properties	Uses
Aluminium	lightweight strength; resists corrosion	building claddings and fittings; light transport; car engines; foil; cooking utensils
Chromium	stainless; resists corrosion	plating steel, brass, etc.; hardening steel alloys and cast iron
Copper	good conductor of heat and electricity; easily bent and shaped	electric wiring and fittings; printed circuits; water-pipes; pots and pans
Gold	soft; does not corrode; good conductor of heat	jewellery; dentistry; electronic circuits; spacecraft reflectors
Iron	strong; cheap	chains and bolts
Lead	soft and heavy; low melting point; resists corrosion; absorbs radiation	weights; printing type; roofing; car batteries; radiation shields
Lithium	lightest metal	light alloys; heart pacemakers
Magnesium	ultra-light but strong; burns easily	car and aircraft parts and engines; cameras; sports equipment; flares; bombs
Mercury	heavy, liquid metal	thermometers; dentistry
Nickel	alloys of nickel resist corrosion and heat stress; low expansion	coins; stainless steel; aircraft engines
Osmium	heaviest metal; makes hard alloys	tips of pens; tools and record styluses
Platinum	resists corrosion and contamination; high melting point	jewellery; laboratory equipment; temperature measurement
Silver	good conductor of heat and electricity; tarnishes in air; reflects light	jewellery; electrical contacts; mirrors; silver plating; photographic film
Tin	soft; resists corrosion	tin plate for cans; used in many alloys
Titanium	strong; resists contamination	air and spacecraft parts; spare-part surgery
Tungsten	hard; very high melting point;	high-speed cutting and drilling tools; electric light filaments; top class darts
Uranium	radioactive	nuclear energy
Zinc	zinc coverings over other metals resist corrosion	coating/galvanizing iron and steel for use in sheeting for buildings; batteries; die cast for Matchbox-type toy cars (though plastic is widely used nowadays)

Alloy	Main metals from which made	Properties	Uses
Brass	copper and zinc	harder than copper; springier than copper; attractive	caps of electric light bulbs; door knobs; bearings and castings
Bronze	copper and tin	harder than copper; easier to melt and cast than copper	used in strips; springs; bells
Gunmetal	copper, tin and zinc	harder than copper; resists corrosion	naval fittings; taps
Pewter	copper, tin and lead	retains colour and finish; most types are easy to shape	ornamental work and jewellery
Solder	lead and tin	soft; low melting point	used to join metals and seal joints
Steel	iron	strong; hard	construction work
Stainless steel	iron, chromium and nickel	resists rusting	knives and forks; surgical instruments

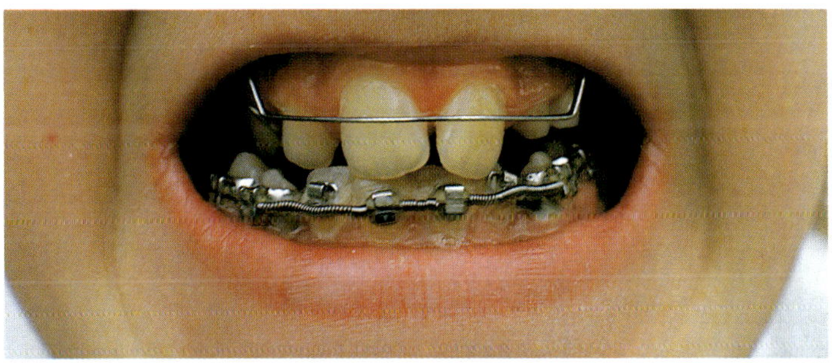

Dental brace

Aeroplane engine

Roadside crash barrier

Brass door fittings

Shaping metals

One of the most useful properties of metal is that it can be turned into almost any shape. The huge lumps, or ingots, of refined metal can become thin, flat sheets, tiny ball-bearings, curly springs or the solid, complicated shape of an engine.

Forging

Some of the red-hot ingots are moved straight to the forge where they are shaped, hammered and pressed into shape before the metal cools and hardens.

Casting

A huge variety of metal objects, from Matchbox-toy cars to real car engines, are made by pouring molten metal into moulds where it cools and sets before the complete object is cast, or tipped out.

Extrusion

Rods are made by extruding, or squeezing, hot metal through a hole, like squeezing out toothpaste from a tube or cake-icing from an icing bag. Hollow tubes are made by squeezing hot, soft metal between the sides of a cylinder and a solid piece in its middle.

Drawing

Fine tubes and wire are made by drawing, or pulling, metal through a series of rollers that squeeze it smaller and smaller.

Continuous casting

This is a modern method of producing enormous quantities of sheet metal. The molten metal pours on to a moving conveyor where it cools and hardens as it travels into the rolling mill. There, it is squeezed between rollers which make it smoother and stronger before it is cut into sections, rolled up and transported to other factories.

(Left) Continuous casting of steel

Bells being cast

These rollers are used in making metal wire. The metal is drawn through the tiny hole between the rollers.

The golden honeycomb

Minos was the legendary King of the island of Crete in the Mediterranean Sea. He kept a hideous monster that devoured young men and maidens. Daedalus was a great craftsman who worked for the King but, after a quarrel with him, Minos imprisoned Daedalus and his son, Icarus. Daedalus asked Minos for their freedom and Minos promised to release them — but only if they performed great acts of skill and craftsmanship. Daedalus made many almost magical things like walking figures with moving arms and open eyes. He also made a golden honeycomb.

1 It seemed impossible that such a delicate, complicated shape as a honeycomb could be made in gold. Taking a honeycomb, Daedalus extracted the honey and put the empty wax comb in a box. He filled every space in and around it with close-packed, fine sand.

2 Then he poured in molten gold. The white-hot gold streamed through the comb, melting the wax and taking its place. When the gold had cooled and hardened, the sand was brushed and blown away. A perfect golden honeycomb had taken the place of the 'lost wax'.

3 Daedalus could even add golden bees by taking dead insects, packing them in sand and replacing the tiny bodies with molten gold.

4 Even after this wonderful creation, though, King Minos would not let Daedalus go. Perhaps you know the story of how Daedalus and Icarus finally escaped with wings of feathers and wax and how Icarus lost his life when he flew too close to the sun?

We still use the 'lost wax' method to make delicate castings. Modern craft workers have succeeded in making a honeycomb of pure gold.

Protecting metals

Our atmosphere contains oxygen, water and carbon dioxide. Most metals can combine with these to form new substances on their surfaces. This process is called corrosion. The form of corrosion you are probably most familiar with is rust. Rust is a reddish-brown coating that occurs on iron and steel. It is made very easily wherever steel meets moist air.

Manufacturers take a lot of care to try to make sure that cars don't rust too quickly. They know that if the car was poorly protected when it was made, no amount of care will stop it rusting in time.

Some car bodies have as many as seven layers of protection put on the bare metal. The steel may be treated with acid, to **etch** the body and help the paints to stick. It must be totally dry, otherwise rust will start to form under the paint. Layers of undercoat, top coat and lacquer are put on. Hollow parts are filled with wax and plastic liners are often put under the wings. **Underseal** is applied and the whole car is cocooned in wax until it is delivered to the garage.

Many manufacturers are so sure of their rust-proofing that they offer a seven-year 'perforation guarantee'. What does that mean? However, even the best rust-proofing won't work if the car is scratched. Why is this?

Some cars are made from glass-fibre or aluminium which are expensive. Bonnets, boots and bumpers are often made of plastic. Why do you think these materials are chosen?

Some metals begin to corrode very quickly so they have to be protected as soon as they are produced. A thin outer coating of paint or 'plate' is added by spraying or dipping the new metal.

Zinc is used to coat, or galvanize, iron and steel. Food cans are plated with tin; screws and fittings are plated with chromium or brass; cutlery with silver and bath taps with 'gold'. In the world of metal, few things are truly what they seem. Some metals are coated with plastic while they are still hot.

Copper and aluminium develop a thin coat of oxide when they are left exposed to the air which prevents any further damage to the metal beneath.

Car being dipped in rust-proofing solution

Electric robots spray-painting cars

Paintwork being finished off

Cars going into a paint-drying tunnel lined with hot electric bulbs

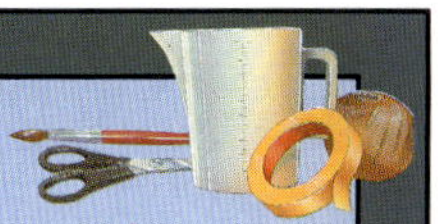

Are there ways of stopping iron and steel rusting — or slowing the process down?

- Try putting steel paper-clips on a dry plastic plate. Put some more on a wet plastic plate.
- Leave them for a few days.
- Do they rust? Which rust first?
- Can you stop the paper-clips rusting? You need to prevent oxygen and moisture from reaching the metal. Try oiling them with cooking oil or wrapping them in clingfilm, for example.
- Can you think of other ways to stop the paper-clips rusting? Test your ideas on the wet and dry plates.
- Try some other metals too — coins, brass paper-fasteners, aluminium foil, for example.

Recycling metals

The demand for metals is growing constantly. In this age of electronics and nuclear energy, machines play an increasingly great part in people's lives. Even inside the human body, pieces of metals can now make vital replacement parts. New materials for special jobs are being created.

The research and development of new materials are very expensive though, and manufacturers and builders need to keep down their costs. Modern cities are being built and re-built all over the world and concrete reinforced with steel rods and mesh is still the cheapest strong material available for building. The number of vehicles on land and in the sea and air increases daily. Soon many more families will have not just one but two 'metal boxes-on-wheels' to drive about the sprawling towns and cities.

Will the Earth be able to provide enough metal for all the needs of the 21st century? There are still huge deposits of metal in several countries but many would be very expensive to mine and transport. Meanwhile, millions of tonnes of scrap metal lie unused, littering the landscape.

Recycling, by collecting, sorting, returning and re-melting scrap metal, is now a vitally important part of the metal industry. In **foundries**, returning offcuts and scrap to the 'melt' is part of the production line routine.

There are several campaigns to encourage people to save unwanted metal. Metal banks now stand alongside bottle banks in many towns. To conserve the Earth's resources and the landscape, it is vital for more metal waste to be salvaged and recycled.

Traffic jam

This pile of rusting wrecks in a scrapyard may soon become new cars again. Some of the parts can be reconditioned and used in other cars. The steel from the wrecks can be recycled and used to manufacture new cars. It is amazing to realize that all the shiny new cars in a car showroom are mostly made from old, recycled metal.

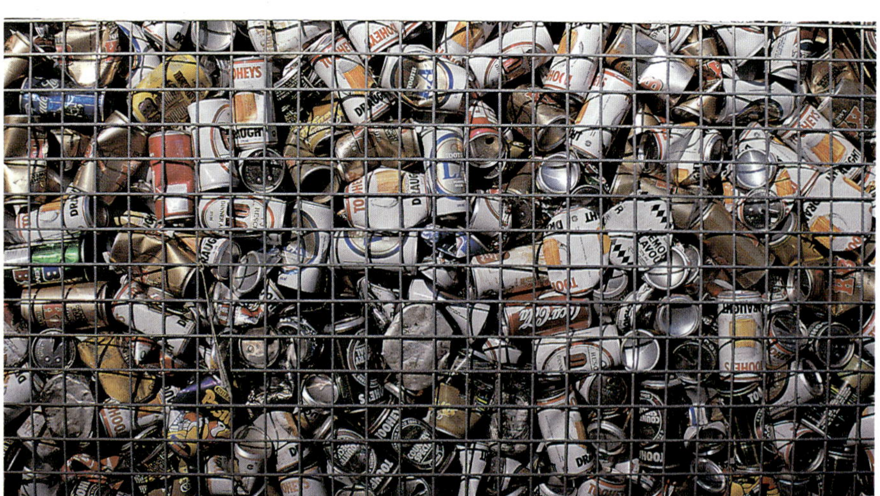

(Left)
Aluminium cans collected for recycling

Metal from scrap cars being shredded

Magnetic crane removing iron and steel from a pile of shredded car bodies

Aluminium foil is collected in huge quantities by organizations which sell it to earn money to train guide dogs for the blind. It costs a lot of money to sponsor a guide dog through its rearing and training period. Several hundred sacks of foil need to be collected to sponsor just one dog.

A great deal of scrap comes from broken-down cars. The 'sink and float' method is used to sort the different metals. After the heavy items like the engine block are removed, the car is shredded, iron and steel are removed magnetically and the remainder is flooded with water. The light debris floats and the metals sink. These are then flooded with other liquids to separate light metals like aluminium, from brass, copper and zinc. Identifying the different metals among scrap is a special skill.

In 1988, nearly six billion drinks cans were sold in the UK. About half of the cans used in the UK are made entirely from aluminium. Fortunately, aluminium drinks cans are very suitable for recycling so an aluminium drinks can recycling programme has been set up. Many fund-raising organizations, including schools, scout and guide packs, hospitals and charities collect cans and receive money back in return.

The story of money

Long ago, people used to trade or barter by exchanging different kinds of goods, such as cattle for corn, or pots for cloth. Then a much more convenient system was introduced in which people used metal tokens or coins in payment for whatever they wanted to buy or sell. These tokens had to be rare, valuable, long-lasting and small so that they were easier to move about than a cow or a fragile pot! Pieces of gold and silver were ideal. Each token or coin was stamped with a symbol so that its value could be recognized. Coins from different tribes or countries were often marked with a portrait of the king or queen.

In the Middle Ages, coins were made by hand. Ingots or bars of special metal such as gold or silver were hammered flat and cut into pieces that were then rounded and stamped with a particular symbol. Their true value was tested by checking the purity of the metal and weighing them. The making, or minting, of coins was strictly controlled. Counterfeiting, which means making false copies, was punishable by death. To prevent people clipping or filing off fragments of coins to melt down, some coins were made with ridged, or milled, edges. Then it was easy to see if part of the coin had been removed.

When a country ran into debt, through having to pay for armies to fight wars, for example, they often made their coins less valuable by using cheaper metal. Today, the value of our coins is no longer related to the value of the metal in them. For over 40 years, our 'silver' coins have had no silver in them at all. Only special collectors' coins are still made with precious metals in them. However, if you find an old ten or five pence piece made before 1947 — an old florin or shilling — it may contain some real silver.

Roman coin

Viking silver penny

Gold and silver coins from the Spanish Armada

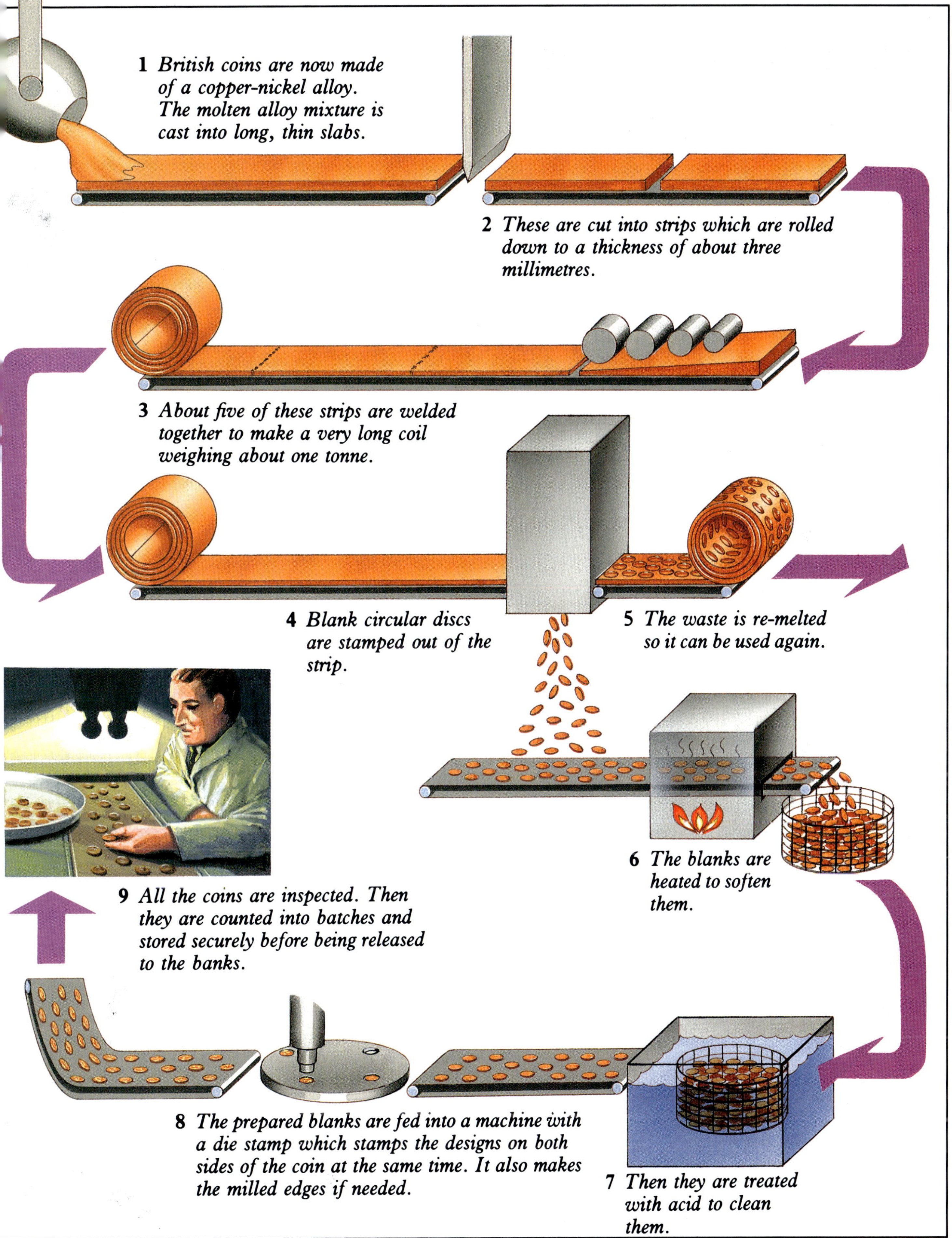

1 *British coins are now made of a copper-nickel alloy. The molten alloy mixture is cast into long, thin slabs.*

2 *These are cut into strips which are rolled down to a thickness of about three millimetres.*

3 *About five of these strips are welded together to make a very long coil weighing about one tonne.*

4 *Blank circular discs are stamped out of the strip.*

5 *The waste is re-melted so it can be used again.*

6 *The blanks are heated to soften them.*

7 *Then they are treated with acid to clean them.*

8 *The prepared blanks are fed into a machine with a die stamp which stamps the designs on both sides of the coin at the same time. It also makes the milled edges if needed.*

9 *All the coins are inspected. Then they are counted into batches and stored securely before being released to the banks.*

Amazing facts about metals

Alchemy

For hundreds of years, some people who were thought to be wizards or sorcerers, practised alchemy. This was a mixture of science, magic and religion. Many alchemists spent years trying to change cheap metal into silver or gold, without success!

Copper

The metallurgical sign for copper is the same as the Egyptian symbol meaning 'eternal life'. The Egyptians knew how long lasting copper can be. An Egyptian water-pipe made of copper was dug up and found to be hardly changed in colour or condition after 5000 years of being buried underground.

The golden fleece

The Greek legend of Jason and the golden fleece is based on true fact. The people who lived on the shores of the Black Sea used to obtain gold by pegging sheep's fleeces in river-beds. As the muddy waters of a river gushed downhill, grains of gold stuck to the greasy, woollen fibres of the fleece.

Aluminium

The statue of Eros in Piccadilly Circus, London, is made of aluminium. Nearly a hundred years old, it has hardly been affected by weathering despite the heavily polluted atmosphere around it.

Napoleon III of France was so impressed by the newly discovered metal, aluminium, that he had a huge set of banqueting cutlery made from it in 1845. At the time, aluminium was more expensive than gold or silver.

The 1906 Rolls Royce Silver Ghost had an aluminium bonnet and aluminium body panels, mudguards and gearbox castings. Car designers are currently seeing how more aluminium could be used in car manufacturing to keep down the weight and save petrol.

Eros

Eiffel Tower

Towers

The tallest tower ever built before television masts came into being was the Eiffel Tower in Paris, France. It was built of iron in 1889. It originally measured 300.5 m tall but with the addition of a radio antenna in 1957, it now measures 320.75 m which makes it higher than the Chrysler Building in New York.

The tallest structure in the world is the galvanized steel Warszawa radio mast in Poland which is 646.38 m high.

Bead of mercury

Mercury

Mercury is a unique metal because it is liquid at ordinary temperatures. It flows so easily that it is sometimes known as 'quicksilver'. Mercury vapour and many substances containing mercury are very poisonous. One effect of mercury poisoning is that the victim starts 'seeing things'. In the past, mercury was used to polish top hats to give them a sheen. The workers involved often suffered from mercury poisoning. Hence the expression, 'as mad as a hatter'!

Mercury is used today in barometers, thermometers, batteries, switches, lamps and other electrical goods. Mercury alloys are used quite safely by dentists for teeth fillings.

The Dump

Across the tip we played,
Where summers ran screaming
On schooldays-end legs
And cogwheels gnawed the cinder path
With hungry teeth of rust. It was there that
Gantries looped their smashed and awry arms
And toppled into pools of ebony oil,
Where cables hissed and slithered in the wind.

All those hot summer days of childhood
The tip smelt of oil and rust and grass.
Great boilers boomed like stranded whales,
Their skin, a dry, red, crispy shingle,
That burst into a flame of copper moths
Beneath the bricks we threw.

Then we left them to their dying;
Watched the birds nest in their clutches,
Those cast-off old machines that grabbed the sky.
The fire weed and the ragwort made their way
Through spokes and ducts and sumps
And flashed green rags of banners in the sun.

My playground was a tip,
My countryside a waste of brick and dust,
Where grass and rain gnawed, picked and bit
As the slowly changing landscape fell to rust.

Mike Harding

Roadside

Beside the road,
Narrow strips of
Field still run,
Full of pale
Grass, thin scrub,
Scrap and rust
Of things
Cast away —
A dead glove,
Empty bottle-skulls,
A shivering spirit
Of lost cellophane.

Valerie Worth

How plastics have replaced metals and other materials

50 years ago

Some people say that we live in the plastics age! We depend on things made from plastic. In fact, we take plastic for granted. But even 50 years ago, there were virtually no plastics. What do you think people used then instead of plastic food coverings, nylon tights, plastic waterproof jackets, plastic toothbrushes, combs, baths, telephones, radios, TVs, shoes and carrier bags? Of course, some of these things did not even exist 50 years ago but what do you think the other things were made from? Mostly, they were made from materials such as wood, cotton, silk, wool, china or metal. Many items are still made from such materials but you can nearly always find a suitable alternative in plastic.

Study these scenes very carefully. How many objects can you spot that are plastic now but that were normally made from other materials 50 years ago?

Now

The Plastics Age

Have you heard of the Stone Age or the Iron Age? These are times in history which have been named after the materials in common use then. In the Stone Age, people made clubs and axes from stone. By the Iron Age, they had learned how to smelt iron to make hard, sharp-edged tools. Perhaps historians in the future will look back on this time when you are alive and call it 'the Plastics Age'.

Look around you now at the room you are in. How many plastic objects can you see? Pens, rulers and pencil cases are often made from plastic; classroom tables may be covered with plastic sheets; even your chair may be plastic; floor tiles, window frames, light switches and light shades are probably plastic; most of the containers in the room are likely to be plastic whether they are rigid, like trays, bottles and jars or flimsy, like crisp and sweet packets.

Then there is the 'hidden' plastic. Plastic can act like another material. For example, clear plastic can act as glass, soft plastic can seem like rubber, and plastic with a shiny surface can be like metal.

Most important of all, plastic threads or fibres can replace cotton or wool or any of the other natural materials that make up our clothes. So, if you look at the labels in your jumper, your tee-shirt or your coat, you may see words like 'nylon', 'acrylic' or 'polyester'. These are artificial fibres.

Some clothes are a mixture of artificial and natural fibres. A tee-shirt or item of underwear can be 'polycotton' — a mixture of polyester and cotton. It will have the qualities of both.

'Plastic' means bendy and supple. It means something that can be moulded. Many substances — clay or wax, for example — are 'plastic'. Nowadays, the word is usually used to describe a range of familiar materials that are made from oil; a range of materials that will take any shape we choose.

Variety of plastic objects

Plastic flowerpots

Acrylic jumpers

/here does all this plastic come from?

o answer that question, we have to go back in time — illions of years back in time — to when the seas were teeming ith tiny green algae and minute animals called plankton. As ey died, their bodies and remains drifted down to the sea-bed nd were buried in the mud there. Over millions of years, they hanged into a thick, black sludge and then into thick, black oil. and and silt collected on top of the sludge, burying and queezing it.

The thick, black oil had once been the remains of plants and nimals. All plants and animals' bodies contain energy — nergy that first came from the sun. Other animals could have aten the algae and plankton and used the energy for life — but hey didn't. The energy was locked up, first in dead animals and lants, then in the sludge and finally in the oil. The sun's energy vas locked up, waiting to be used.

People have known about oil for thousands of years — it is aid that Noah used thick, black pitch which comes from oil to vaterproof the Ark. Nowadays, oil is used in many different vays. Oil can be quite solid or runny like syrup. The oil that omes straight out of rock is called crude oil. Crude oil is drilled for all over the world, on land and at sea. It usually has to be **refined** into different parts before it can be used at all.

Different parts are used for different purposes. Some are ideal for lubricating, others such as petrol and paraffin give off tremendous energy when they are lit. Some parts are light, explosive gases, others make thick, heavy road surfaces.

Part of the crude oil — about one-tenth — is made up of complicated chemicals that scientists can change from a gas or liquid to a bag of hard, shiny granules. These colourless granules are what we call plastic. Plastic can be coloured, melted, squashed or stretched, rolled into sheets or pulled into fibres. New ways of using plastic and new types of plastic are being found all the time.

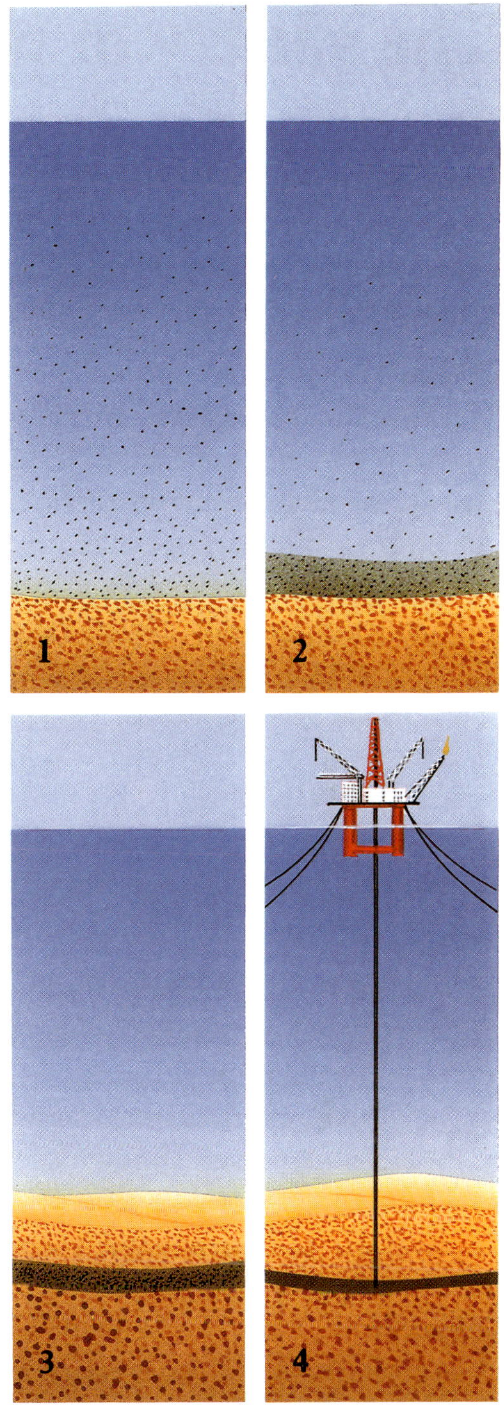

Raw plastic granules made from oil

Tarmac road surface made from oil

The variety of plastics

There are so many different kinds of plastic and they have so many different uses, that it is hard to recognize and group them. Most have very long names that describe the complicated chemicals that make them up. We use some of these names every day — nylon, polythene and polystyrene, for example.

Rope made from artificial fibres

Nylon

Nylon is strong and light. It can be moulded or made into sheets. Most important of all, it can be stretched into long, strong filaments. Such filaments are used to make strong bristles for brushes and mats or tough ropes and racquet strings. Fine nylon filaments can be made into delicate stockings or woven into bullet-proof vests. Nylon filaments can be **crimped** to produce a thick and bulky material that traps air and makes a good insulator when used in a jumper or coat. Nylon is resistant to decay — it won't rot away. Moulded, solid nylon is very tough and wears slowly. This nylon makes good shoe heels or gears, especially gears that have to run without being oiled. Lots of toys and models have nylon gears.

Tennis rackets with nylon strings

PVC

PVC is short for the chemical name, polyvinylchloride. It has some particularly useful qualities: it is waterproof and it is an excellent insulator of electricity.

PVC can be pressed into delicate things like long-playing records; moulded into sturdy road traffic cones; or coated on to electrical wire. Your 'rubber' wellies may be PVC; a shiny raincoat will be coated with PVC; school bags and luggage may be made from PVC sheet. If you have ever jumped on a big inflatable like a bouncy castle, you have jumped on PVC fabric.

PVC wellingtons

(Left)
Bouncy castle made from PVC

olystyrene

olystyrene can be a hard, rigid material. It is made into food ontainers, yoghurt pots and model kits. It has a smooth surface nd can be cut, glued and painted. However, it is fragile — as ou will know if you have dropped something like a model eroplane.

You may also find polystyrene as an 'expanded' material. The ackaging for delicate objects or the thick insulating layer inside cool-box is made from this light, soft material. Expanded olystyrene can be broken easily; it can be cut and shaped with ot wire. It may also feel warm to the touch — it reflects back our body warmth to your hand. This is why it is good for eeping things hot or cold.

Expanded polystyrene packaging

olythene

olythene is a tough, light plastic that can be moulded and haped. Buckets, bowls and some furniture may be made from olythene. Polythene sheets can be made into bags and sacks. olythene is a good electrical insulator and can cover wires and witches.

Polythene takes around 40 years to decay, when it becomes rittle and crumbles. This is fine for electrical wires which stay safe for a long time but not such good news when we come to throw polythene objects away. Adding starch, a natural white substance found in bread and potatoes, to polythene, makes a plastic that breaks down in less time — around eight years.

Polythene buckets and containers

Acrylic

Acrylic can be made into hard, often clear, materials like car lamps, spectacle lenses and telephones — or into soft fibres that help to make natural materials hard-wearing and crease-resistant.

Heating and folding acrylic fibres can make them into a bulky material that traps air in coats and jumpers, insulating you and keeping you warm.

Acrylic car headlamps

Shaping plastics

Plastic can be shaped when it is hot. This is a very useful quality.

Many plastics can be rolled into thin sheets when they are hot. Heavy metal rollers roll out the plastic like a rolling-pin on pastry. Then the sheet can be cut and joined, sometimes by welding which involves heating and squeezing the sheets together. Look at polythene bags and the cover on your teacher's Ginn Science file.

Plastic can be heated, pressed and moulded. Bowls and buckets can be made this way. Plastic granules or powder are put into a hot mould and squeezed into shape while hot. The shaped bowl is popped out of the mould by an ejector. It may need trimming before it is used.

Sometimes, hot, molten plastic is squirted, or injected, into a closed mould. After it has cooled, the mould is opened and the hardened pieces can be removed.

Lots of small plastic parts can be made at the same time. The plastic is squirted into tunnels that branch into the small pieces. When the plastic has cooled, the parts can be broken off the sprue which is the tree-like shape that joins them. The sprue can be melted and used again. If you buy a model kit, the small parts may have been left on the sprue; you break or cut them off as you use them.

Hollow plastic shapes, like bottles, are made by putting a tube of hot plastic into a mould. When the mould is closed, air is blown into the tube which swells like a balloon, shaping itself against the mould. When the mould is opened, the plastic has become a bottle.

Polythene sheeting being rolled and cut

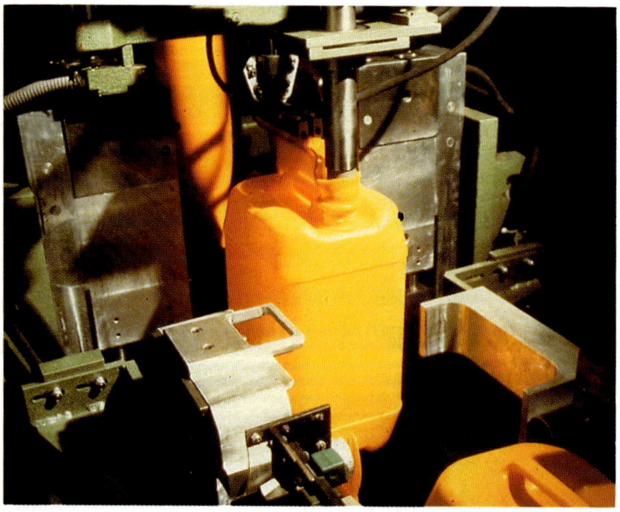

(Left)
This machine makes plastic containers by blowing a hot plastic tube into the shape of a mould.

Machinery for making plastic bottles

Plastic foam is made by mixing chemicals inside a mould. When they are mixed and warmed, they swell up to 30 times their original size, filling the mould. When they have cooled and set, the chemicals have become a light, soft, plastic foam.

Some thin sheet shapes, like the packaging inside a box of chocolates, are made by vacuum-forming. Sheets of warm, soft plastic are put over a mould. Then the air is sucked out of the mould, pulling the sheet down into it. When the plastic cools, it has taken the shape of the mould.

The moulds to make plastic shapes are very complex and very expensive to make. It may cost tens or even hundreds of thousands of pounds to produce the mould for something as complex as a camera body. Even the moulds for *LEGO* are very expensive; each *LEGO* brick must be perfect or it won't link to make a good model.

Manufacturing plastic drainpipes

Polythene tubing being extruded

Legoland

Testing plastics

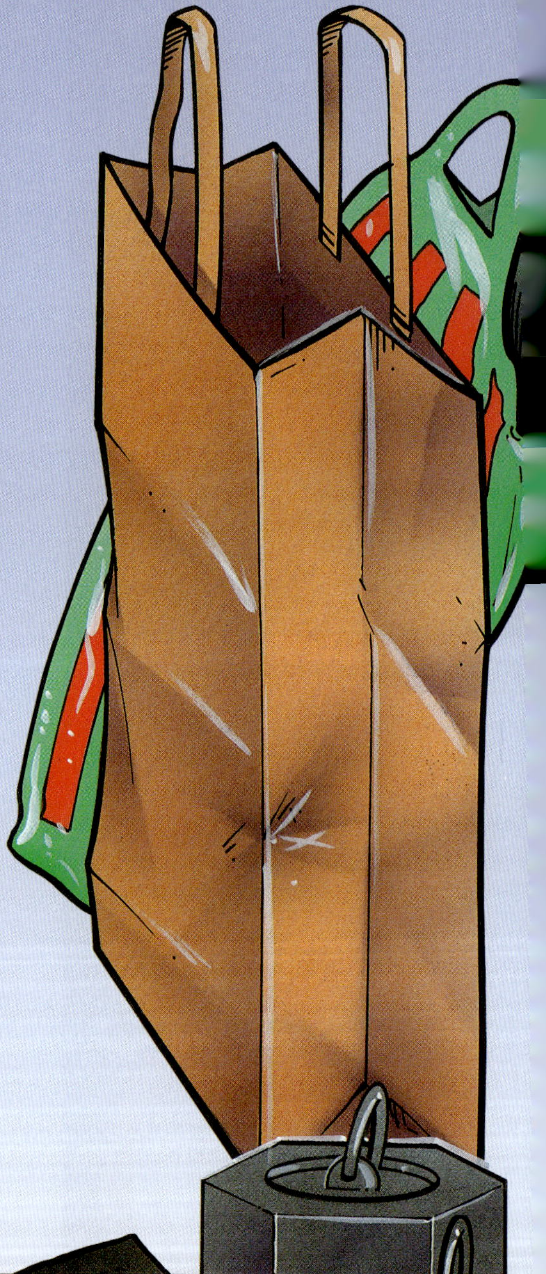

Plastic bags
Many plastic bags are designed for particular uses. Some shops have specially shaped bags for carrying pot plants home, for example. Others have bags for carrying suits and skirts. Rubbish bags are large and strong.

- Collect a variety of bags and examine them. What special qualities does each bag have? How is each bag particularly suited to its job?

Have you tried carrying shopping in a large paper bag with handles? What about a large plastic bag with handles?

- Find out which type of shopping bag is stronger. Look at all parts of each bag — the sides, the bottom, the handles and the seams.
- Would it make any difference if it were raining and the bags became wet? Test this.

Collect plastic carrier bags from different shops.

- Devise a test to find out which shop supplies the strongest bag.

When carrying a fully loaded bag, your hands can become marked by the handle pulling down on your skin.

- Carry out a test to discover which bag has the handle that will mark your hand least.

Here are some things which might help you carry out your tests:

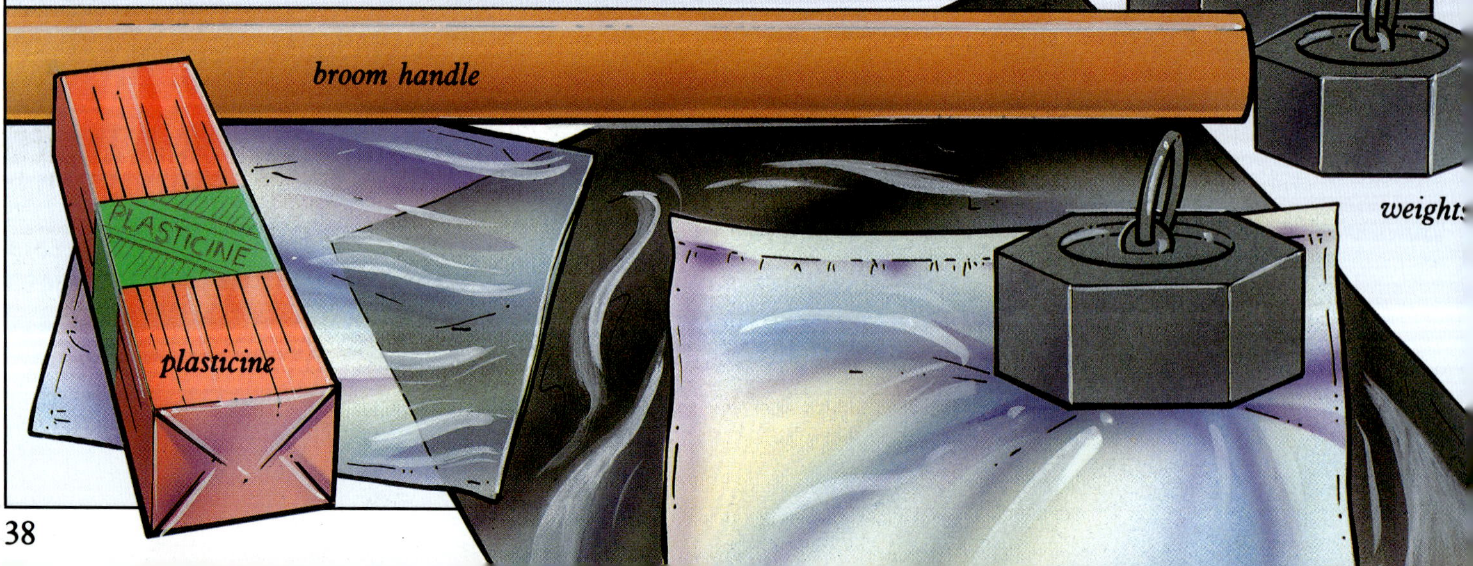

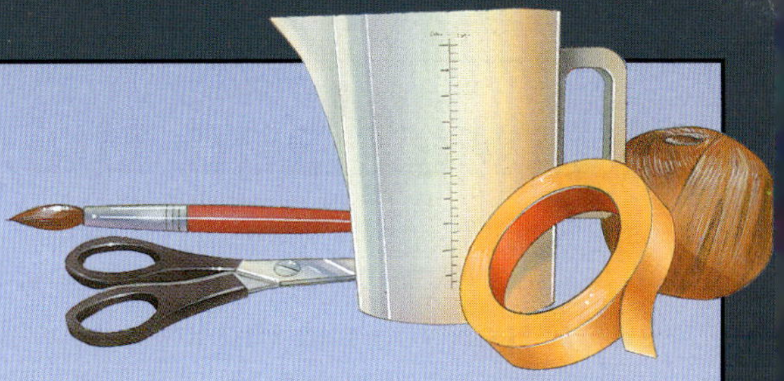

Keeping things cold

- Devise a test to compare how different materials keep things cold.

Here are some things which might help you carry out your tests:

Egg-boxes

- Find out if eggs are better protected in clear plastic egg-boxes, polystyrene egg-boxes or cardboard egg-boxes.

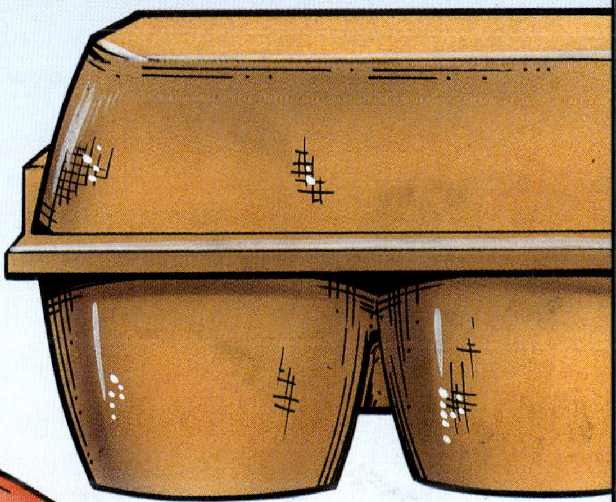

Plastics and the environment

Plastics seem to be in use almost everywhere. Make a list of all the uses you can think of. Plastics can be strong, flexible and light. Most importantly, plastics last a long time.

Plastics which don't wear out are a great help to us in many ways; imagine if the plastic gears on your bike were to wear out every two or three days. But they also bring problems. Take a look at a nearby rubbish dump. Paper bags or cardboard containers begin to rot away quite quickly but the plastic bags, yoghurt pots and plastic sheets seem to stay there forever. Unfortunately, many people still don't realize how ugly and dangerous litter is. Look at the sides of roads and in the corners of playing fields. Crisp packets, plastic drinks bottles, chocolate wrappers and polythene bags are particularly visible and lie there until somebody can clear them up.

A group of plastics called thermoplastics can be melted and re-used time after time. Acrylic and nylon are both thermoplastics. The main problem with recycling plastics is that there are so many different types that it would be almost impossible to separate everything that is thrown away. Also, some plastics can't be melted down and re-used. These are called **thermosetting** plastics. Melamine, used for plates, and urethane, used for electrical work, are two of the thermosetting plastics.

The strength and durability of plastic is one of its major advantages for making things that will last. When we use plastics to make things we normally throw away though, we are left with the problem of how to get rid of it all.

Plastic pollution, particularly from the plastics which can't easily be re-used, is a growing problem. Scientists developing new plastics are trying to find ways in which plastics will decompose naturally. Shops near you may have begun to use plastic bags which will disintegrate after a period of time. Others are trying to encourage people to buy fairly cheap but strong plastic bags that can be used many times, rather than giving away free plastic carriers which are only used once then thrown away. There is still a lot of work to be done, though.

You can help now by thinking carefully about where you throw your plastic rubbish away. Remember, wherever you leave it, it is likely to be there for a long time. Never drop litter of any kind — always find a litter bin or take it home to throw away.

Artificial fibres

A fibre is any thread-like strand of a substance. There are hundreds of uses for fibres and each fibre has its own particular qualities which are suitable for different jobs. You might want a fibre to be absorbent, hard-wearing, elastic or a combination of all of these.

Fibres can be made from natural products or they can be made artificially. Natural fibres such as cotton and flax come from plants; others, such as fur and hair, come from animals.

Artificial fibres are usually made from plastic. To make an artificial fibre, the molten plastic is squeezed through a series of tiny holes in a machine. As it emerges from the holes (called spinnerets), the plastic cools into the thread-like strands.

Plastics are made from different combinations of chemicals. As the chemicals are mixed in varying degrees, a different plastic is made with a particular set of strengths and weaknesses. So, when the qualities a particular fibre needs have been identified, the right combination of chemicals is chosen for the plastic. Nylon fibres are lightweight and strong; polyester fibres are durable and regain their shape easily; acrylic fibres are soft and durable.

Artificial fibres have become more and more common. They can be made to a particular recipe and they can be available when and where required. You will probably find them most often in your clothes, in your furniture at home and in various forms of insulation although they have hundreds of other uses too.

Artificial fibres are so common that over two-thirds of all the fibres used in the USA are now artificial. Natural fibres will still continue to be used, though. They have their own special qualities which means they are often preferred to artificial fibres.

Carpets made from artificial fibres

(Right)
The space suits worn by astronauts are made from artificial fibres.

Fibre '66'

All the clothes people wore, all carpets, curtains, sheets, chair covers, tents, parachutes and fishing lines, used to be made out of things which grew naturally. Wool from sheep, cotton from the cotton plant, linen from the flax plant, hair from camels and goats, silk spun into small, egg-shaped, yellow cocoons by silkworms. 'Artificial' fabrics called rayon and acetate were invented at the end of the last century by British chemists but they were made from natural things, like woodpulp, which had been treated with chemicals.

Then, in the laboratories of an American chemical company, scientists invented a totally new material. This new material could be woven into a fabric even lighter than silk but it was extremely tough. It formed a fibre stronger, weight for weight, than steel wire. It could make bristles for toothbrushes, sails for ships and ropes for tying them up. It could be spun into strands or rolled into flat sheets. It didn't burn — it melted. It could stretch and spring back to its original shape. It didn't go mouldy and moths didn't eat holes in it.

This miracle material, the scientists proudly announced in October 1938, was made from some of the most common things found on Earth: coal, water and air. So the basic building blocks were just carbon, oxygen, hydrogen and nitrogen. People could hardly believe the reports . . .

But the simple ingredients hid a story of many years of careful and difficult work by scientists and of expensive research and development.

1 In the 1920s, the chemical and explosives manufacturing company, Du Pont, employed teams of scientists to research new products to make and sell. In 1930, a scientist working in the Du Pont laboratories was heating some chemicals together into a sticky mass when he noticed something odd. The substance could be stretched into long threads. After cooling, the threads could be stretched more, and yet they became stronger.

This substance was in fact the first synthetic fibre. Unfortunately, the strange thread softened in hot water so Dr Wallace Carothers, the man in charge of the research team, decided to concentrate on looking for a better, more useful fibre. He mixed and tested a new group of chemicals. He almost gave up. Nothing seemed to work. One thread would melt at a low temperature, another broke easily. But gradually, he found a group of chemicals which showed promise. Du Pont picked what they thought was the best.

2 Much testing was now necessary. What could the new material really do? What could it be used for? The scientists at Du Pont were very excited. They had created a truly 'synthetic' fibre — something made in the laboratory, not found in nature — which looked as if it could have hundreds of uses.

But the new material was only really useful if it could be manufactured cheaply, in huge quantities. The scientists could make it in small quantities. Now they had to find out how to make it in factories.

New, complex machinery had to be designed to produce the fibre. Ways of colouring it and turning it into the things the public would buy had to be invented.

A name had to be found for the new substance too. Its real name was polyhexamethyleneadipamide. Du Pont called it *Fibre '66'*. But it needed a name which people all over the world could use and pronounce easily. A committee met over the months to consider names.

3 Someone suggested Norun, then Nulon, then Nilon and eventually . . .

4 On 27th October 1938, Du Pont introduced nylon as the name for this amazing new fibre.

Dr Wallace Carothers, the inventor of nylon. A shy, sensitive man, he died in 1937 aged 41 just after he had applied for a patent on artificial fibres. His work also led to the invention of artificial rubber and the family of artificial fibres called polyesters.

5 What should be the first things made from nylon? Du Pont tried out a batch of toothbrushes made with nylon bristles. They made nylon fishing line and nylon thread for surgeons to use instead of silk. But their big plan was to provide women with nylon for their legs, as stockings. In the past, stockings had been made of wool, cotton or rayon which were not particularly attractive. The most attractive stockings were made of Japanese silk but they were very expensive.

6 The first experimental nylon stockings were sold to Du Pont employees in February 1939. On 15th May 1940, five million pairs of nylon stockings were put on sale in shops all over America.

7 The stockings sold out on the first day. Women rushed to buy nylon stockings which were much cheaper than silk stockings. Now most women could afford to look as if they were wearing silk on their legs. Yet nylon was tougher, it washed easily and it dried quickly. And the material could be made in America. Du Pont struggled to supply enough nylon fibre to spin into the new, see-through, shiny stockings. They built more factories.

When the United States entered the econd World War in 1942, all nylon vent to military use. Nylon stockings ecame glamorous luxuries of the past. Iere is part of a report written in July 945 about the way nylon was being ised by American servicemen fighting n the Pacific region.

Nylon's Life-saving War Jobs

FLAK CURTAINS - woven into the strongest fabric for its weight ever made, nylon hangs in curtains in the interior of bombers to stop flak.

HUMAN PICK-UP DEVICE - Nylon rope, strong, lightweight and elastic, is used in the new human pick-up device that makes it possible for a plane to swoop down and snatch up a wounded man without stopping.

Unlike other textile fibres, nylon is not affected by the Pacific humidity because it is non-absorptive and dries quickly. Termites don't care for it. So thousands of yards of olive-drab nylon netting and screening are going as head-nettings, hammock canopies and screening for barracks, tents and hospitals.

Nylon goes into hammocks and lightweight ponchos. It weighs less than cotton and has a tensile strength almost twice as great.

PARACHUTES - Millions of yards of finely woven nylon fabric float gently to Earth carrying their precious human cargo to safety when men bale out of planes.

FLYING SUITS of nylon guard against death from insect bites or sunburn when men are forced down. These suits provide a lightweight covering for the entire body, comfortable even in the tropics.

BOMBER AND FIGHTER PLANE TYRES are built around plies of nylon cord. This makes them heat resistant, stronger yet lighter, and able to withstand the strain of landing tremendous weight at high speed on jagged, improvised fields.

More than 1.5 million PAINT BRUSHES made with nylon bristles have been supplied to the Navy. These bristles replace hog bristles that formerly came from the Orient, wear at least three times longer.

9 When the war ended, nylon could be used to make stockings again. Police controlled huge queues in America.

10 The many uses developed for nylon in the war carried on into peacetime. Nylon was made into clothes, underwear, curtains, carpets, ropes, nets, parachutes, combs, brushes, luggage, seat-belts, hoses, moving parts in machinery and much more. Nylon began to be so much a part of everyday life that people took it for granted.

Other synthetic fibres were invented, such as acrylics and polyesters. But nylon was the world's first, commercial, truly synthetic fibre.

Fantastic plastic

Plastics have amazing properties. They can be used in extraordinary ways. Plastic can even be used to make joints to replace our worn-out bones. New uses are being discovered all the time; perhaps you will find some too!

Reflective clothing

Plastic for reflection

Look at the reflectors on your bike. They are made of plastic and they catch and reflect the light, shining brightly in the dark whenever a light falls on them. Tiny plastic **prisms** coat road signs and cinema screens, making them reflect the light from headlamps or the film projector. Before these were available, film screens were sometimes kept wet with a constant shower of water to reflect the light better and make the film clearer.

Plastic for leather

Leather is an expensive material to buy. Many people object to wearing leather because it is the skin of a dead animal. Plastic can take the place of leather but it doesn't usually let air in. So feet in plastic shoes will get hot and sweaty. Some plastics do let air in. They are made by squeezing plastic fibres together. A thin polythene layer on the outside gives a shiny finish, like real leather.

Artificial heart made from plastic and metal

Plastic for life

Our heart is designed to last — literally, for life. In our lifetime, it will beat and pump blood millions of times. But some parts of the heart may wear out, especially the valves and the big tubes called arteries. Surgeons can replace these with plastic valves and plastic tubes, giving people longer and more active lives.

Carpet clues

Plastic carpets made with nylon or acrylic carry tiny electric charges when they are brushed by our feet. These little charges may stay on the carpets for days. So, if tiny plastic beads are scattered on the carpet, they are attracted to the charge. They will show where any footprints are and help the police to find and identify them.

The instant igloo

Polyurethane foam is made by mixing small quantities of two chemicals together and heating them. They bubble and expand to 30 times their original size. Polyurethane foam can be shaped in moulds to make seat cushions and mattresses. A more rigid type of polyurethane is often used in structures like aircraft wings.

An arctic survival pack has been made which includes the chemicals used to make polyurethane, a heating unit and a plastic bag shaped like an igloo. When the fuel is lit, the chemicals expand and fill the plastic bag 'mould' to produce an instant igloo, two metres in diameter with ten centimetre thick walls.

Polyurethane foam being cut

Powerful plastic

The rocket-heads and fuel-tanks on spaceships are often made from plastic. A special kind of plastic is used that is ten times harder than steel and can stand up to the incredible heat that occurs around a space-craft re-entering the Earth's atmosphere.

Bulletproof plastic

Kevlar is a plastic that can be woven into an immensely strong material which is hard to cut or tear. Kevlar jackets are bulletproof and are often worn by soldiers and members of the police force for protection.

Soldier wearing a bulletproof jacket

Shrinking plastic

If you put old crisp packets or plastic wrappers from chocolate bars on to a baking tray and into an oven set at a low temperature for a few minutes, they shrink to a fraction of their original size. They still keep all their print but they become stiff and thick. Use a paper-punch to put a hole in one end and loop a metal ring through. You have made a handy key-ring!

What you have actually done is reverse the process that made the original wrapper when sheets of plastic were heated, rolled and stretched before being printed and cut.

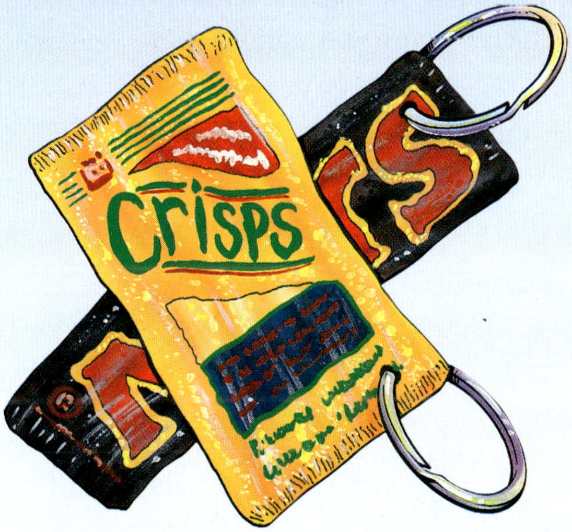

Only try this with an adult present.

Glossary

alloys
An alloy is a metallic substance made up of a mixture of two or more metals or a metal and another substance.

crimped
To crimp something is to press it into small ridges or folds.

etch
To etch something is to inscribe or engrave its surface. Acid is often used to do this.

filaments
A filament is a long, thin strand. Filaments in light bulbs are the thin wires which become white hot and give off light.

foundries
A foundry is a place where metals are melted and then hardened in moulds to make objects.

metallurgists
A metallurgist is someone who studies the structure and properties of metals.

oxide
An oxide is a substance made up of oxygen and another substance.

panning
Panning is the process of separating gold from gravel by swilling the mixture with water, round and round, so that the gravel floats off leaving the gold.

prisms
A prism is a block of glass or other transparent material, usually with a triangular base.

refined
To refine something is to make it purer.

smelt
To smelt is to extract a metal from an ore by heating it.

thermosetting
Thermosetting plastics are ones which have been hardened by heating and moulding.

underseal
Underseal is a plastic-type covering applied to the under surface of motor cars to protect them from corrosion.

Index